AMAZING ANIMALS
OF THE WORLD 1

Volume 1

Aardvark — Bobcat

GROLIER
an imprint of
SCHOLASTIC
Scholastic Library Publishing
www.scholastic.com/librarypublishing

First published 2008 by Grolier, an imprint of Scholastic Inc.

For information address the publisher: Grolier, Scholastic Library Publishing
90 Old Sherman Turnpike
Danbury, CT 06816

Printed and bound in the U.S.A.

Library of Congress Cataloging-in-Publication Data
Amazing animals of the world 1.
v. cm.
Contents: v. 1. Aardvark-bobcat — v. 2. Bobolink-cottonmouth — v. 3. Coyote-fish, Siamese fighting — v. 4. Fisher-hummingbird, ruby-throated — v. 5. Hyena, brown-mantis, praying — v. 6. Marmoset, common-owl, great horned — v. 7. Owl, pygmy-robin, American — v. 8. Sailfin, giant-spider, black widow — v. 9. Spider, garden-turtle, common musk — v. 10. Turtle, green sea-zebrafish.
Includes bibliographical references and index.
ISBN 0-7172-6225-1; 978-0-7172-6225-0 (set : alk. Paper) - ISBN 0-7172-6226-X; 978-0-7172-6226-7 (v. 1 : alk. paper) - ISBN 0-7172-6227-8; 978-0-7172-6227-4 (v. 2 : alk. paper) - ISBN 0-7172-6228-6; 978-0-7172-6228-1 (v. 3 : alk. paper) - ISBN 0-7172-6229-4; 978-7172-6229-8 (v. 4 : alk. paper) - ISBN 0-7172-6230-8; 978-7172-6230-4 (v. 5 : alk. paper) - ISBN 0-7172-6231-6; 978-0-7172-6231-1 (v. 6 : alk. paper) - ISBN 0-7172-6232-4; 978-0-7172-6232-8 (v. 7 : alk. paper) - ISBN 0-7172-6233-2; 978-0-7172-6233-5 (v. 8 : alk. paper) - ISBN 0-7172-6234-0; 978-0-7172-6234-2 (v. 9 : alk. paper) - ISBN 0-7172-6235-9; 978-0-7172-6235-9 (v. 10 : alk. paper)
1. Animals—Encyclopedias, Juvenile. I. Grolier Incorporated. II. Title: Amazing animals of the world one.
QL49.A453 2007
590.3—dc22
2007012982

About This Set

Amazing Animals of the World 1 brings you pictures of 400 exciting creatures, and important information about how and where they live.

Each page shows just one species, or individual type, of animal. They all fall into seven main categories, or groups, of animals (classes and phylums scientifically) identified on each page with an icon (picture)—amphibians, arthropods, birds, fish, mammals, other invertebrates, and reptiles. Short explanations of what these group names mean, and other terms used commonly in the set, appear in the Glossary.

Scientists use all kinds of groupings to help them sort out the thousands of types of animals that exist today and once wandered the earth (extinct species). *Kingdoms, classes, phylums, genus,* and *species* are among the key words here that are also explained in the Glossary.

Where animals live is important to know as well. Each of the species in this set lives in a particular place in the world, which you can see outlined on the map on each page. And in those places, the animals tend to favor a particular habitat—an environment the animal finds suitable for life—with food, shelter, and safety from predators that might eat it. There they also find ways to coexist with other animals in the area that might eat somewhat different food, use different homes, and so on.

Each of the main habitats is named on the page and given an icon, or picture, to help you envision it. The habitat names are further defined in the Glossary.

As well as being part of groups like species, animals fall into other categories that help us understand their lives or behavior. You will find these categories in the Glossary, where you will learn about carnivores, herbivores, and other types of animals.

And there is more information you might want about an animal—its size, diet, where it lives, and how it carries on its species—the way it creates its young. All these facts and more appear in the data boxes at the top of each page.

Finally, the set is arranged alphabetically by the most common name of the species. That puts most beetles, for example, together in a group so you can compare them easily.

But some animals' names are not so common, and they don't appear near others like them. For instance, the chamois is a kind of goat or antelope. To find animals that are similar—or to locate any species—look in the Index at the end of each book in the set. It lists all animals by their various names (you will find the Giant South American River Turtle under Turtle, Giant South American River, and also under its other name—Arrau). And you will find all birds, fish, and so on gathered under their broader groupings.

Similarly, smaller like groups appear in the Set Index as well—butterflies include swallowtails and blues, for example.

Table of Contents
Volume 1

Glossary

Amphibians—species usually born from eggs in water or wet places, which change (metamorphose) into land animals. Frogs and salamanders are typical. They breathe through their skin mainly and have no scales.

Arctic and Antarctic—icy, cold, dry areas at the ends of the globe that lack trees but are home to small plants that grow in thawed areas (tundra). Penguins and seals are common inhabitants.

Arthropods—animals with segmented bodies, hard outer skin, and jointed legs, such as spiders and crabs.

Birds—born from eggs, these creatures have wings and often can fly. Eagles, pigeons, and penguins are all birds, though penguins cannot fly through the air.

Carnivores—they are animals that eat other animals. Many species do eat each other sometimes, and a few eat dead animals. Lions kill their prey and eat it, while vultures clean up dead bodies of animals.

Cities, Towns, and Farms—places where people live and have built or used the land and share it with many species. Sometimes these animals live in human homes or just nearby.

Class—part, or division, of a phylum.

Deserts—dry, usually warm areas where animals often are more active on cooler nights or near water sources. Owls, scorpions, and jack rabbits are common in American deserts.

Endangered—some animals in this set are marked as endangered because it is possible they will become extinct soon.

Extinct—these species have died out completely for whatever reason.

Family—part of an order.

Fish—water animals (aquatic) that typically are born from eggs and breathe through gills. Trout and eels are fish, though whales and dolphins are not (they are mammals).

Forests and Mountains—places where evergreen (coniferous) and leaf-shedding (deciduous) trees are common, or that rise in elevation to make cool, separate habitats. Rain forests are different (see below).

Freshwater—lakes, rivers, and the like carry fresh water (unlike Oceans and Shores, where the water is salty). Fish and birds abound, as do insects, frogs, and mammals.

Genus—part of a family.

Grasslands—habitats with few trees and light rainfall. Grasslands often lie between forests and deserts, and they are home to birds, coyotes, antelope, and snakes, as well as many other kinds of animals.

Herbivores—these animals eat mainly plants. Typical are hoofed animals (ungulates) that are common on grasslands, such as antelope or deer. Domestic (nonwild) ones are cows and horses.

Hibernators—species that live in harsh areas with very cold winters slow down their functions then become inactive or dormant.

Invertebrates—animals that lack backbones or internal skeletons. Many, such as insects and shrimp, have hard outer coverings. Clams and worms are also invertebrates.

Kingdom—the largest division of species. All living things are classified in one of the five kingdoms: animals, plants, fungi, protists, and monerans.

Mammals—these creatures usually bear live young and feed them on milk from the mother. A few lay eggs (monotremes like the platypus) or nurse young in a pouch (marsupials like opossums and kangaroos).

Migrators—some species spend different seasons in different places, moving to where more food, warmth, or safety can be found. Birds often do this, sometimes over long distances, but other types of animals also move seasonally, including fish and mammals.

Oceans and Shores—seawater is salty, often deep, and huge. In it live many fish, invertebrates, and some mammals, such as whales and dolphins. On the shore, birds and other creatures often gather.

Order—part of a class.

Phylum—part of a kingdom.

Rain forests—here huge trees grow among many other plants helped by the warm, wet environment. Thousands of species of animals also live in these rich habitats.

Reptiles—these species have scales, have lungs to breathe, and lay eggs or give birth to live young. Dinosaurs are thought to have been reptiles, while today the class includes turtles, snakes, lizards, and crocodiles.

Scientific Name—the genus and species name of a creature in Latin. For instance, *Canis lupus* is the wolf. Scientific names avoid the confusion possible with common names in any one language or across languages.

Species—a group of the same type of living thing. Part of an order.

Subspecies—a variety but quite similar part of a species.

Territorial—many animals mark out and defend a patch of ground as their home area. Birds and mammals may call very small or very large spots their territories.

Vertebrates—animals with backbones and skeletons under their skins.

Aardvark
Orycteropus afer

Length of the Body: about 3½ feet
Length of the Tail: about 2 feet
Weight: 132 to 176 pounds
Diet: mainly termites; also other insects

Number of Young: 1
Home: Africa
Order: aardvarks
Family: aardvarks

 Grasslands

 Mammals

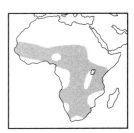

The aardvark is unlike any other creature on Earth. But it shares the traits of several common animals. Its body is like a pig's. Its long, muscular tail is like that of a kangaroo. Its snout is similar to an anteater's. The aardvark's most unusual feature is its long, sticky tongue. The animal uses it to find termite nests. It then laps up the tasty insects. The aardvark's teeth are also unique. Human teeth are covered with enamel. An aardvark's teeth are not. So they wear down easily. But this is not a problem for the animal. Its teeth keep growing throughout its life.

Aardvarks were never very common. Many years ago, they lived in Africa. Today they inhabit only the grasslands and savannas south of the Sahara desert. There they dig long burrows in the soft soil. During the day, aardvarks sleep alone or in pairs. They rest in underground tunnels. These tunnels do not contain nesting materials. There is just some loose dirt left from days of digging. The creatures come out an hour or two after the sun goes down. They begin their hunt for termite nests at this time.

The female aardvark gives birth once a year to a single baby. When it is three weeks old, the youngster follows its mother out of the nest. It begins to hunt for food. Lions, leopards, and hyenas are the aardvark's main enemies. Pythons sometimes enter the burrows to eat the young.

Wandering Albatross
Diomedea exulans

Length: 44 to 48 inches
Wingspan: 11 feet
Weight: up to 26 pounds
Diet: fish
Number of Young: 1

Home: oceans in the Southern Hemisphere
Order: auks, herons, and relatives
Family: albatrosses, fulmars

 Oceans and Shores

 Birds

© WINFRED WISNIEWSKI / FRANK LANE PICTURE AGENCY / CORBIS

Wandering albatrosses are among the largest seabirds. For months at a time, they fly over the ocean without setting down on land. Their huge wingspan makes them excellent gliders. These birds hold their outstretched wings stiffly. If winds are strong, they can glide for hours without flapping their wings. They land on the ocean surface to feed and to drink salt water.

Albatross eat mainly fish, which they grab with their long, thick bill. This bill has a powerful hook at the tip that makes capturing prey easy work. Albatross also follow ships and feed on garbage tossed overboard. The birds live over the southern oceans. There icebergs are common and winds are often very cold. But their thick coat of feathers keeps them warm. The feathers are mainly white with black tips on the wings.

Wandering albatross venture onto land only to breed. They usually nest in colonies on small islands. Both parents build the nest, using moss and mud. The parents take turns sitting on the one large egg. The egg weighs about a pound and must be incubated for more than two months. The baby bird is covered with soft down feathers and cannot fly. It needs several months of care before it can fly out to sea and search for food on its own. During this period the parents come and go. They return to the nest two or three times a week, bringing food to their offspring.

American Alligator
Alligator mississippiensis

Length: 6 to 19 feet
Weight: about 550 pounds
Diet: fish and other small vertebrates
Number of Eggs: 20 to 80

Home: southern United States
Order: crocodiles, caimans, and relatives
Family: alligators, caimans

 Freshwater

 Reptiles

© GEORGE MCCARTHY / CORBIS

There are only two known species of alligator in the world. One lives in China. The other lives in the southeastern United States. This one is called the American alligator. Both species live on riverbanks and in swamps. In the past, the American alligator was quite common. It was hunted for its scaly skin. Expensive handbags, shoes, and wallets are made from this skin. Selling alligators as pets also decreased their numbers. Legend has it that young alligators were brought to New York. They were flushed down toilets and ended up in the sewers. They supposedly multiplied. There is no proof that this actually happened. But the story lives on.

Young alligators eat shellfish and insects. As they grow, they attack fish, frogs, rodents, birds, and sometimes deer. But they are not a real danger to people. An alligator spends most of its time completely still, warming itself in the sun. Alligators mate in the water. The female builds a large nest on a riverbank. She lays from 20 to 80 eggs and covers them with rotting plants. As the plants continue to rot, they make heat. This keeps the eggs warm. Two or three months later, the eggs hatch. The young call to their mother, who opens the nest. The young alligators soon begin to feed themselves.

American alligators have been protected from hunters since the 1960s. They have made a remarkable comeback.

Green Anaconda
Eunectes murinus

Length: up to 33 feet
Weight: about 440 pounds
Diet: animals weighing up to 100 pounds
Number of Young: 11 to 50
Length at Hatching: 2 to 3 feet

Home: Trinidad and South America
Order: scaled reptiles
Family: boas, boids

  Freshwater

Reptiles

© FRANCOIS GOHIER / PHOTO RESEARCHERS

The green anaconda is the largest snake in South America. This reptile is a powerful swimmer. It lives in and around streams, forests, and ponds. The anaconda is the world's only giant water snake. It spends much of its time hiding among reeds and lily pads. In this way, it avoids the few animals bold enough to attack it. The anaconda also uses its cover to sneak up on prey. Its favorites are fish, ducks, and animals drinking from the water's edge. This immense creature spends much of its time hanging over tree branches, sunning itself.

The anaconda is like its cousin, the boa constrictor. Both kill their prey by holding it tightly in their jaws. Then they wrap their long body around it and squeeze. But the anaconda does not crush its prey. It suffocates it. When the prey exhales, the anaconda squeezes more tightly. Soon the animal cannot breathe at all and dies.

Anacondas can swallow very large animals. In fact, they can eat so much in one meal that they don't need to eat again for more than a year! But an overstuffed anaconda may find it hard to move. This leaves it open to attack by human predators. Anacondas rarely attack humans. They only do so in self-defense.

Angelfish
Pterophyllum scalare

Length: 6 to 8 inches
Diet: fish, insects, and plants
Length: 6 to 8 inches
Number of Eggs: up to 1,000

Home: South America
Order: perch-like fishes
Family: cichlids

 Freshwater

 Fish

© MARK SMITH / PHOTO RESEARCHERS

Angelfish are beautiful creatures. They live in the rivers of South America. Angelfish are also popular aquarium pets. Some aquarium angelfish are all black or all white. Some angelfish have many other markings.

Male and female angelfish share in the care of their babies. In rivers, they prepare for parenthood by cleaning an area of the riverbed. They find a spot with leafy underwater plants. The female fish places her eggs on the leaves. Then the male fertilizes the eggs. Using their fins, the parents fan the eggs with streams of fresh water. If an egg-eating fish appears, the parents quickly move the leaf holding the eggs to safety. The female angelfish usually takes care of the eggs. She will seldom flee the nest when predators attack.

When their eggs are ready to hatch, the parents chew at the shells to help the young come out. Tiny newborn angelfish are called "wrigglers." They cannot swim until they are four or five days old. During this time the parents continue to fan and clean them. For several more weeks, even after the wrigglers start swimming, the parents protect their young from predators.

American Anhinga
Anhinga anhinga

Length: 32 to 36 inches
Wingspan: up to 48 inches
Weight: up to 3 pounds
Diet: mainly fish
Number of Eggs: 1 to 5

Home: southern United States, Central America, and South America
Order: auks, herons, and relatives
Family: anhingas

 Freshwater

 Birds

© JAMES ZIPP / PHOTO RESEARCHERS

The American anhinga is also called the snakebird. This is because it has a very long, "snaky" neck. This lovely bird often sits on tree branches at the edge of rivers, ponds, marshes, and other bodies of fresh water. There it patiently watches for fish. When an American anhinga spots its meal, it dives into the water and spears the fish with its long, pointed bill. The anhinga returns to the water's surface, flips the fish into the air, and catches it as it falls, swallowing it headfirst. Anhingas also eat crayfish, water snakes, aquatic insects, turtles, and other small animals.

An American anhinga often swims low in the water. Only its head and neck are above the surface. Sometimes it swims underwater with its wings partly spread. Unlike ducks and geese, the anhinga does not have waterproof feathers. After an anhinga is in water for a while, it must go onto land and spread its wings to dry the feathers.

American anhingas nest in small colonies near water. They often nest together with herons and egrets. They build nests of sticks on the ground or on tree branches overhanging the water. The nests are lined with soft moss and cypress leaves. The male anhinga gathers the nesting materials and carries them to his mate, who makes the nest. The two parents take turns guarding the nest and incubating the eggs, and both parents care for the young birds.

Army Ant
Eciton burchelli

Length: 1 inch
Diet: mainly wasps, ants, and other insects
Number of eggs: 100,000 to 300,000

Home: from southern Mexico to Brazil and Peru
Order: ants, bees, wasps
Family: ants

 Rain Forests

 Arthropods

There are hundreds of different kinds of army ants. They share an interesting behavior. They move in long columns—just like soldiers. They attack insects, spiders, and almost any other animal that crosses their path. One species is *Eciton burchelli*. It lives in moist tropical forests. An *Eciton* colony has 700,000 ants.

Ants in an *Eciton* colony march and stop. A march lasts about 17 days and occurs at night. During the day the ants camp and search for food. Workers capture prey and carry it back to the camp. Large soldier ants go with the workers. They stand ready to defend them against attack. At the end of the march, the ants camp in one area for about 20 days. During this time, the queen lays up to 300,000 eggs. The eggs soon hatch into larvae. A few days later, larvae born during the previous stop become adults. Then the colony begins to move again. As the colony marches, special nurse ants carry and feed the larvae.

Army ants can be very harmful to animals and crops. But they are also useful. They destroy such pests as cockroaches and bedbugs during their journeys.

Black Carpenter Ant
Camponotus pennsylvanicus

Length: ¼ to ½ inch; queen can be much larger
Diet: insects, fruit juices, and sugar
Method of Reproduction: egg layer

Home: central and eastern North America
Order: ants, bees, wasps
Family: ants

 Forests and Mountains

Arthropods

© E. R. DEGGINGER / ANIMALS ANIMALS / EARTH SCENES

Carpenter ants are hard workers whose specialty is wood. Unfortunately, they cause a lot of damage. They often live inside wooden beams of buildings, old logs, tree trunks, and poles. They don't eat the wood. Instead, they build tunnels through it. This weakens the structure and may cause it to fall apart.

The carpenter ant's natural home is the forest. Over the years they have moved into suburban areas across North America. Once inside a home, the large colonies hide within walls and roofs. No one usually notices them until their damage is done. The carpenter ant's tunnels form miniature cities. Thousands of worker ants live as a colony.

Carpenter ants are social insects. They work, eat, and breed as a group. A single, large queen usually heads a colony. Her main job is to lay eggs. She is taken care of by a troop of female ants who don't breed. These workers tend to the nest. They defend it from enemies. And they take care of the eggs. Only a small number of male ants are born in the nest. Their main job is to fertilize a new queen.

Carpenter ants like to eat a sugary liquid called honeydew. This is produced by another insect, the aphid. The ants look after the aphids. Both species benefit from the relationship. The ants get food. And the aphid is protected from predators.

Fire Ant
Solenopsis geminata

Length: ¹⁄₁₀ to ¼ inch
Diet: seeds and insects
Method of Reproduction: egg layer
Home: southern North America, Central America, the Caribbean islands, northern South America, and tropical Africa and Asia
Order: ants, bees, wasps
Family: ants

Have you ever been bitten by a fire ant? Then you know how it got its name. Why does the fire ant's bite sting so badly? It is because of a strong venom in the insect's jaw. Fire ants use their powerful venom against other kinds of ants, with which they often battle. In addition to venom, fire ants produce chemicals. They uses these chemicals to communicate with each other. Fire ants leave chemical trails along the ground to lead their brothers and sisters to food. They release other chemicals into the air to tell each other when it is time to fight or to retreat.

During the 1500s fire-ant populations on some Caribbean islands were very high.

Spanish settlers were forced to flee in their boats. Two hundred years later, fire ants became a big problem on the island of Grenada. Government leaders offered a reward of 20,000 English pounds to anyone who could get rid of them. Fire ants are pests not only because of their sting. They also eat the seeds of crops and many wild plants and cause permanent damage.

In the United States, the native fire ant is much less of a problem than two other species of fire ants that recently arrived from South America. The South American fire ants are more aggressive. They have pushed the native fire ant out of its former grassland home.

nteater

phaga tridactyla

of the Body: 3¼ to
eet
th of the Tail: 2¼ to 3
eet
eight: 65 to 75 pounds
Diet: ants, termites, and beetle
larvae

Number of Young: 1
Home: northern and central
South America
Order: edentates
Family: American anteaters

 Grasslands

 Mammals

© THEO ALLOFS / ZEFA / CORBIS

Imagine eating 35,000 insects every day! That's what the giant anteater does. This huge animal feeds on tiny creatures. Its favorites are ants and termites. The giant anteater has adapted to help it catch and eat prey. Its strong legs have claws that are 6 inches long. The anteater uses these claws to tear open rotting logs, large anthills, and termite nests. The anteater's head ends in a long, pointed snout. It has no teeth. They aren't needed to eat ants. The creature has a slender tongue. It may be up to 2 feet long. And it is coated with lots of sticky saliva. The anteater whips the tongue in and out of its mouth to lick up ants.

At night and after a big meal, the giant anteater curls up to rest. It spreads its big, bushy tail over its body. In this position, it looks like a pile of dead leaves. This helps the anteater hide from pumas, jaguars, and other enemies.

Giant anteaters live alone except when courting and mating. A female carries a baby for about six months. The baby weighs about 2½ pounds at birth. The mother nurses the baby for about three months. She teaches the young anteater how to find and eat ants. The mother walks about or swims across a river. And she carries the baby on her back the whole time.

Giant anteaters live in savannas, swamps, and forests. Hunting and farming have greatly reduced their numbers.

Archerfish
Toxotes jaculatrix

Length: 9 inches
Diet: flies, winged termites, cockroaches, and other insects; spiders
Method of Reproduction: egg layer

Home: Asia
Order: perch-like fishes
Family: archerfishes

 Freshwater

Fish

© JERRY YOUNG / DK LIMITED / CORBIS

The remarkable archerfish catches its dinner by spitting at its prey! It shoots a thin jet of water at an unsuspecting insect that may be crawling on a leaf or twig. It knocks the victim into the water, where it can be caught and eaten. The archerfish is an accurate spitter. It rarely misses anything less than 3 feet away. If the fish does miss a target, it quickly shoots again. The archerfish can even hit prey 10 feet away.

Archerfish learn to spit when they are only about 1 inch long. They can spit only small drops at first. And their aim is poor. But they become experts with practice. Some people keep archerfish in aquariums. There they show off their amazing shooting skills on unlucky flies or crickets.

This fish can also live in all kinds of environments. It lives in salt water, fresh water, and brackish water. Brackish water is a mixture of salt water and fresh water. Archerfish are often found swimming and hunting in brackish water at the mouth of a river. The fish swims near the water's surface among shoreline reeds. Often the tip of its mouth is just above the water. Its large eyes help it scan the surroundings for its favorite targets. These include flies, termites, cockroaches, caterpillars, and spiders. For variety the archerfish also dines on small crustaceans and other water animals.

Screaming Hairy Armadillo
Chaetophractus vellerosus

Length of the Body: 9½ to 10 inches
Length of the Tail: about 4 inches
Weight: 12 to 17 pounds
Diet: insects, dead animals, roots, and fruits

Number of Young: unknown
Home: central South America
Order: edentates
Family: armadillos

 Grasslands

 Mammals

© OLIVER BERG / DPA / CORBIS

The word *armadillo* is Spanish for "armored one." This describes these bony-plated animals. The hairy armadillos are recognized by their straggly coats of long, bristly fur. The screaming hairy armadillo is the smallest of its kind. It is the only armadillo to make a sound. It screams in terror when attacked by a predator such as a hungry fox.

Armadillos are the only mammals in the world to grow bony armor. They are born soft and pink. Soon after birth, the baby armadillo's leathery skin becomes covered with scales. Under these scales grow many small, hard plates that expand and eventually join together. The armor completely protects the armadillo's head, shoulders, back, and pelvis. Its belly, however, remains soft and vulnerable to attack. The armadillo's armor also helps the animal dig through the earth. The hairy armadillo is the fastest digger in its family. It can disappear into the ground in seconds. All armadillos can hold their breath for up to six minutes, even while digging furiously. This ability helps the armadillo keep dirt out of its throat and lungs.

While other armadillos remain hidden in their burrows, hairy armadillos often emerge to hunt. They can be seen in broad daylight, waddling across grasslands and sand dunes. These creatures seldom bother to return to their old burrows, but simply dig new ones when it's time to sleep.

Asp
Vipera aspis

Length: 20 to 30 inches
Diet: mice, moles, shrews, lizards, and frogs
Number of Young: 4 to 18

Home: central and southern Europe
Order: scaled reptiles
Family: pit vipers, vipers

 Forests and Mountains

 Reptiles

© O. ALAMANY & E. VICENS / CORBIS

An asp lies very still and watches carefully. This is how it hunts. When a mouse, lizard, frog, or other prey comes close, it strikes. It sinks its two sharp fangs into the victim's flesh. The asp's large glands contain venom, or poison. The venom flows through the fangs and into the wound. If the prey escapes, the venom soon slows it down. The asp follows the prey's scent. It eventually catches up to the dying animal. Then it grabs the animal and slowly swallows it whole.

The asp is a good hunter. But it is not an aggressive snake. When it senses danger, it quietly—and quickly—hides in a dense bush or under a rock. It strikes and bites only when it is stepped on or senses danger.

Asps may be gray, brown, red, or all black. The markings also vary. Some asps have small spots or lines on their back. Others have a zigzag pattern. Asps live in different kinds of habitats. But they prefer crevices and other hiding places.

After two asps court and mate, the eggs stay inside the female's body. At hatching time, the eggs open inside the mother. The young are born live. Newborn asps can care for themselves. Their mother does not care for them. They soon crawl away to establish their own territories.

African Wild Ass
Equus asinus

Length of the Body: about 6½ feet
Length of the Tail: 17 inches
Height at the Shoulder: 4 to 5½ feet
Weight: about 600 pounds
Diet: grass, bark, and leaves

Number of Young: 1
Home: Africa
Order: odd-toed hoofed mammals
Family: asses, horses, and zebras

 Deserts

 Mammals

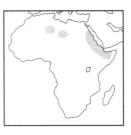

© TOM BRAKEFIELD / CORBIS

? Endangered Animals

African wild asses once covered all of northern Africa. Scientists know this from studying buried bones. Today only a few thousand animals survive.

Ancient people hunted the African wild ass. But they valued the animal too much to harm an entire herd. African sultans allowed people to kill only a few animals. They believed that parts of the animal could cure some illnesses. The wild ass's problems arrived with the automobile. Modern hunters chased herds across desert plains. Hunters shot many of these animals. Dozens more died of exhaustion from the chase.

The African wild ass can survive the harsh African climate. The animal gets moisture from grasses and plants. During the dry season, it stays near a spring or river. When it rains, herds may travel many miles.

The domestic donkey comes from the African wild ass. Escaped donkeys often mate with wild asses. This reduces the number of true African wild asses born each year. Fortunately, the government of Ethiopia is protecting a few large herds in national parks.

Aye-Aye
Daubentonia madagascariensis

Length of the Body: 18 inches
Length of the Tail: 22 inches
Weight: 4½ pounds
Diet: fruits and insect larvae

Number of Young: 1
Home: Madagascar
Order: primates
Family: aye-ayes

 Rain Forests

 Mammals

© NIGEL J. DENNIS / GALLO IMAGES / CORBIS

? Endangered Animals

Aye-ayes hold the unfortunate distinction of being the world's most endangered primate. The native people of the island country of Madagascar, the only place on Earth where these creatures are found, have cut down the forests where the aye-ayes have lived for thousands of years. Even worse, these same people kill any aye-ayes they see, owing to a superstition that claims these animals are somehow evil.

In its native habitat, an aye-aye is difficult to spot. It sleeps during the day, curled up in a ball with its tail draped over its body like a blanket. The aye-aye is most active at night, but even then it rarely emerges from its home high in the trees, where the leaves provide good camouflage.

To find its favorite food—insect larvae—an aye-aye taps on trees with its long middle finger. Scientists believe that the aye-aye can hear changes in vibration. A cavity containing insect larvae sounds different than solid wood. When an aye-aye locates food, it chews through the bark and uses its middle finger to pull out the larvae.

To save the aye-aye from extinction, scientists are trying to breed the animals in captivity—a task that has proven difficult. But in 1992 Blue Devil was born at the Duke University Primate Center in North Carolina. Blue Devil was the first aye-aye born in captivity outside Madagascar in 100 years.

Chacma Baboon
Papio ursinus

Length of the Body: 2¼ to 3½ feet (male); 1½ to 2½ feet (female)
Length of the Tail: 14 to 32 inches
Weight: up to 75 pounds

Diet: various plants and animals
Number of Young: 1
Home: southern Africa
Order: primates
Family: Old World monkeys

 Grasslands

 Mammals

© NIGEL J. DENNIS / GALLO IMAGES / CORBIS

A group of chacma baboons arrives at a favorite drinking hole. Most of the members bend down to drink the fresh water. But other members act as lookouts. They watch for leopards, eagles, and other enemies. If they see any enemy approaching, they warn the rest of the baboons by screeching and running around in circles.

Members of a chacma baboon group help one another in other ways. If one baboon is wounded, the others will take care of it. They'll also help each other during fights with other animals.

The chacma is a large baboon with dark fur. Its black face has a very long, narrow muzzle. Small eyes are situated below a prominent forehead ridge. The creature's arms and legs are sturdy and of equal length. All four limbs are used for walking, running, and climbing. The chacma spends most of its time on the ground, though it sleeps in trees. This baboon eats many different foods. Some of its favorites are grasses, seeds, fruits, nuts, roots, invertebrates, and small mammals. Chacmas that live on seacoasts also eat mollusks and crustaceans.

The chacma baboon has two cheek pouches, which open beside the teeth of the lower jaw. A chacma can stuff a lot of food into these pouches. This is very helpful when gathering food in dangerous places. The chacma can quickly cram food into the pouches, then retire to a safe place to eat.

Gelada Baboon
Theropithecus gelada

Length of the Body: 1½ to 2½ feet
Length of the Tail: 12 to 20 inches
Weight: 31 to 46 pounds
Diet: plant matter, fruits, and small animals

Number of Young: 1
Home: Ethiopia
Order: primates
Family: Old World monkeys

 Forests and Mountains

 Mammals

? Endangered Animals

© GALLO IMAGES / CORBIS

The name *gelada* comes from an Arabic word meaning "collar," or "mane." It refers to the male gelada's impressive cloak of long fur, which flows over his shoulders and halfway down his back. Geladas are also called red-breasted baboons—they sport a crimson patch of skin on their chest.

Geladas live in a treeless world, either on or near a steep, rocky cliff. Huge troops of up to 400 geladas climb up the face of a rock wall to sleep in safety. They climb down in the morning to eat grass on the mountain meadow. The baboons never stray far from the cliff, because the rocks are their refuge should danger appear. The geladas are timid baboons that are easily frightened—for good reason. They are a favorite food of leopards, and humans shoot the males for their thick fur. Within their large troops, geladas live in close-knit families of one male with many female mates and children. But this harem is quite unlike those of other baboons, because the male gelada does not bully or threaten his females. On the contrary, it is the female geladas that form a new family. They then "invite" one male to join their little group.

Geladas have a peculiar way of saying "hello." It's called the lip-flip and involves curling the upper lip over the nose. The shiny pink skin under the lip can be seen many yards away.

Hamadryas Baboon
Papio hamadryas

Length: 24 to 20 inches
Diet: plants, small animals, and honey
Home: the Horn of Africa and the Arabian Peninsula

Order: primates
Family: Old World monkeys

 Grasslands

 Mammals

© GERARD LACZ / ANIMALS ANIMALS / EARTH SCENES

In ancient times, the hamadryas baboon was common in Egypt. People then thought it was the living form of the sun god Toth, and the animal was often shown in paintings and statues. When they died, these baboons were wrapped like mummies and placed in tombs.

In the past, hamadryas baboons formed very large troops that often damaged crops. In the late 1800s, however, the hamadryas was nearly killed off by European hunters. Today there are none left in Egypt, but some can still be seen in the Horn of Africa and the Arabian Peninsula. Hamadryas baboons live in family groups made up of one adult male and one to nine females with their young. At night, these small groups get together as a troop to sleep. As many as 700 baboons may rest on one cliff. In the morning the small groups of hamadryas separate to look for food. Their diet is varied and includes grass, leaves, bulbs, insects, and small animals. Sometimes it even includes such large mammals as hares and young gazelles.

Of all the baboons, the hamadryas lives the farthest east. It lives in the Arabian Peninsula as well as in Africa. All other baboons live only in Africa. In Ethiopia, the hamadryas baboon lives near the Red Sea. Rocky coasts, dry plains, and hilly regions make up its environment. It rarely climbs trees, but it can move well in rocky areas.

Yellow Baboon
Papio hamadryas

Length: 13 to 33 inches
Weight: 18 to 55 pounds
Diet: mostly plant matter
Number of Young: 1

Home: central Africa
Order: primates
Family: Old World monkeys

 Grasslands

 Mammals

© MARTIN HARVEY / CORBIS

Yellow baboons live in well-organized groups. Groups have from 10 to 100 individuals. Members of the group protect and help one another. Females spend their whole lives in their birth group. Males usually leave their birth group when they become adults. Then they move from group to group.

Yellow baboons spend most of their waking hours on the ground. They sleep in acacia trees at night. If acacia trees are scarce, the baboons sleep in rocky areas. It is hard for enemies to reach these places.

During the day baboons search for food. They dig up roots and pick berries. They break off tender stems and scrape lichen off rocks. Most of their diet is plant matter. But yellow baboons also eat animals without backbones. And they dine on young birds and small mammals. Yellow baboons may travel 10 miles or more during the day. At night they settle down to rest. As they travel, females and their young stay in the center of the group. Young males walk along the edge of the group. They act as lookouts for possible danger.

Yellow baboons often travel with herds of impalas or other antelope. The baboons have excellent eyesight. The antelope have an excellent sense of smell. Together the animals know when a leopard, lion, or other predator is near.

Eurasian Badger
Meles meles

Length of the Body: 2 to 3 feet
Length of the Tail: 5 to 9 inches
Weight: up to 55 pounds
Diet: plant matter and small animals

Number of Young: 1 to 6
Home: Europe and Asia
Order: carnivores
Family: badgers, otters, skunks, weasels, and relatives

 Forests and Mountains

 Mammals

© R. PACKWOOD / OSF / ANIMALS ANIMALS / EARTH SCENES

Eurasian badgers are excellent builders. They use their broad feet and long claws to dig underground homes. Their homes have many tunnels and rooms at different levels below the surface. These underground homes are just like the upstairs and downstairs in a house. Badgers work at making their homes larger and adding new entrances and exits. A home can be 90 feet in diameter. It is usually lived in for many years, by generation after generation of badgers.

Badgers live in a variety of habitats. They are common along the edges of forests and in thick brush near fields. They even live in dry, semidesert regions. People rarely see badgers because the animals spend the day resting in their burrows. They come out at dusk to hunt for food. They depend on their excellent sense of smell to locate dinner.

Eurasian badgers eat almost anything they can find. In summertime, badgers weigh between 15 and 30 pounds. In fall, they eat a lot of food, and they almost double their weight. The stored fat helps them to survive cold winters, when finding food is difficult.

Eurasian badgers are playful animals that often scurry about like kittens, jumping and leaping over one another. They mate in summer, and females give birth the following spring or summer. The babies weigh about 3 ounces at birth and are born blind. They do not open their eyes until they are about a month old.

Spiny Bandicoot
Echymipera kalubu

Length: 8 to 20 inches
Length of the Tail: 2 to 5 inches
Weight: up to 4½ pounds
Diet: insects and fruits
Number of Young: 2

Home: New Guinea and New Zealand
Order: marsupials
Family: New Guinea bandicoots, rain forest bandicoots

 Rain Forests

 Mammals

© DANIEL HEUCLIN / BIOS / PETER ARNOLD, INC.

Until recently, very little was known about the habits of the spiny bandicoot, a very common animal on the islands of New Guinea and New Zealand. They are nocturnal and live deep in forests, so few people have ever been able to watch them go about their daily routine. In order to finally learn how spiny bandicoots live, scientists used a very clever method. They trapped 12 of the animals and attached spools to their back. Each spool contained almost a mile of thin, light thread. When the bandicoots were released, the thread left a trail that revealed where the animals had gone.

The thread unraveled by the bandicoots was particularly tangled around fallen trees, suggesting that the animals spend much of their time in these places. Most likely the bandicoots find food among vegetation. The thread suggested that the animals are most active around fruit trees and between rotting logs that teem with tasty beetle grubs.

The scientists also saw evidence that bandicoots take short naps during the night. The telltale threads were often found snarled around clumps of grass that looked as though the bandicoots had rested on them. The thread also led scientists to a better understanding of the nesting and sleeping habits of these nocturnal creatures. Some bandicoots live in burrows under the ground. Others live in hollow logs or under piles of leaves.

Great Barracuda
Sphyraena barracuda

Length: 6 feet
Weight: 83 pounds
Diet: fish
Method of Reproduction: egg layer

Home: eastern United States, southern Brazil, Bermuda, and the Caribbean
Order: perch-like fishes
Family: barracudas

 Oceans and Shores

 Fish

© STEPHEN FRINK / CORBIS

The great barracuda is the giant of the barracuda family. It is one of the most feared predatory fish. It swims very fast and feeds greedily on fish. It charges through schools and attacks with snapping bites. People are interested in this fish because of its behavior. It is known to attack humans. But the threat is probably exaggerated. The barracuda identifies its prey by sight rather than smell. Sudden movement attracts it. Only about 40 human attacks have been reported. All of these occurred in murky waters.

The great barracuda is shaped like a torpedo. It is found in most tropical and subtropical waters. It does not swim in the eastern Pacific Ocean or in the Mediterranean Sea. But it is found mainly along the southern Atlantic coast. The barracuda can change its color to match its environment. Usually, it is deep green to steel gray on top. And it has silvery sides and a white belly. Dark bars appear on the sides of the adults. It has a jutting lower jaw. And its vicious-looking fangs can cut through great lumps of flesh.

The great barracuda is a good food fish. Still, it has not become a seafood favorite. This is largely because the flesh is sometimes poisonous. Poisonous barracuda flesh seems to develop most often in larger, older individuals.

Striped Bass
Morone saxatilis

Length: 1 to 6 feet
Weight: typically 3 to 35 pounds; the record is 125 pounds
Diet: fish, squid, crabs, and worms

Number of Eggs: 1 million to 5 million
Home: North America
Order: perch-like fishes
Family: temperate basses

 Oceans and Shores

 Fish

© TOM MCHUGH / PHOTO RESEARCHERS

Striped bass spend most of their lives in the ocean. But like salmon, striped bass swim up freshwater rivers and streams each year. They do this in order to mate and lay eggs. The journey is necessary because the tiny eggs cannot survive in salt water. The female lays eggs when she is four or five years old. While she lays her eggs, as many as 50 males will surround her and try to fertilize them. The hatchlings instinctively know to swim downstream toward the ocean. They travel in large groups called schools. As they mature, the young bass leave the group and venture out on their own. Striped bass usually swim among rocks close to shore.

Originally, striped bass lived only in the waters along the eastern coast of North America. But about 100 years ago, the fish became very popular for food and sportfishing. So hundreds of them were transported by train to San Francisco Bay and released. The fish thrived there and spread up and down the Pacific coast. Striped bass are now found in many parts of the continent. But they are disappearing from their original home. Pollution and overfishing are reducing their numbers in the Atlantic Ocean. In response, the U.S. government has restricted the number that can be caught by fishermen. The striped bass was the first animal ever to be protected by a law in North America. In 1639 the Massachusetts Bay Colony banned the wasteful use of striped bass as fertilizer.

Asiatic Black Bear
Ursus thibetanus

Length: 6 feet
Weight: 140 to 330 pounds
Diet: fruits, buds, invertebrates, and carrion
Number of Young: 2

Home: Iran, Indochina, Japan, India, Pakistan, Korea, and Southeast Asian islands
Order: carnivores
Family: bears

 Forests and Mountains

 Mammals

© J. M. LABAT / PHONE / PETER ARNOLD, INC.

The Asiatic black bear is also known as the moon bear. It has a white mark on its chest shaped like a crescent moon. The rest of its long, thick fur is jet black. Many strange stories have developed about this beautiful creature. The people of Hainan (a Chinese island) say that the bear sucks its paws when hungry. There are tales that it eats children. And some say its gallbladder moves to different parts of its body depending on the season. Because of these stories, it is called "the terror of the mountain people." The Asiatic black bear is still hunted and killed today because of these false tales.

In truth, Asiatic black bears are shy creatures. They prefer to eat acorns, fruits, and insects. They live a solitary life high in the mountain forests. In the Himalayas, these bears will climb high in the mountains to avoid humans. Yet a few have attacked and eaten cattle. If cornered, the Asiatic black bear can kill a human. But this does not happen often.

The Asiatic black bear is an excellent climber. It has five short, curved claws on each paw. The animal uses them to grip tightly as it climbs. It is also quite agile and can balance on high branches. This ability has made the Asiatic black bear a popular circus performer. However, its favorite activity is sleeping. It spends most of its time snoozing in the hollow of a tree, a cave, or a rock crevice.

Black Bear
Ursus americanus

Length: 4½ to 6 feet
Weight: 200 to 600 pounds
Diet: omnivorous
Number of Young: 1 to 3

Home: North America
Order: carnivores
Family: bears

 Forests and Mountains

 Mammals

© KENNAN WARD / CORBIS

The black bear lives two different lives, according to the season. In the spring, summer, and fall, it thinks only about eating. It can be seen on the shore of a stream or lake fishing for salmon. Black bears are fond of tree resin. They strip the bark of conifers. And they destroy some trees in the process. These foods are not the most important part of their diet, however. Their usual diet is 25 percent rodents and 75 percent plants.

When winter approaches, the bear goes back to its den and falls asleep. During the two to four months of cold weather, the bear's body temperature and breathing slow down. It lives in slow motion! But this is not true hibernation. When the weather gets warmer, it wakes up for short periods. During these breaks it eats a little and gets back its strength. A solitary animal, the black bear lives in an area of 1 to 36 square miles. Mating season is from May to July. In January or February the female gives birth to one to three nearly naked bear cubs. Each one weighs no more than 10 ounces. They do not leave their mother to hibernate in their own area until the second winter.

Its awkward way of walking makes us forget that the black bear is an agile animal. It climbs, runs, and swims well. It rarely attacks people unless it is wounded. But a mother bear with her cubs will attack if she senses danger.

Brown Bear
Ursus arctos

Length: about 8 feet
Weight: 500 to 850 pounds (males)
Diet: mostly large mammals and fish, but some fruits

Number of Young: 2 to 4
Home: northern temperate and Arctic regions
Order: carnivores
Family: bears

 Forests and Mountains

 Mammals

© KENNAN WARD / CORBIS

The brown bear lives in northern Europe, Asia, and North America. There are several types of brown bears. The one found in most of the United States is called the grizzly. Its weight, size, and strength are remarkable. But the grizzly is not the largest bear alive. The Kodiak bear, which lives in Alaska, is bigger. It weighs up to 1,000 pounds. And it can be as tall as 9 feet. The grizzly was widely hunted in the 1800s. Trappers who caught one were greatly admired. There were about 100,000 of them in the early 1900s. Now there are only about 1,000 left.

Grizzly bears eat roots and berries, animal meat, fish, insect larvae, young deer, rodents, and even livestock. They live in large, open spaces. Adult males can inhabit up to 400 square miles. These areas overlap with those of black bears. Violent fights sometimes break out between the two kinds of bears. Grizzly bears have been known to attack when humans disturb them. The grizzly is more at peace with its own kind. And it is the most sociable of the North American bears.

From May to June, males fight for females. These fights rarely end in death. A male mates with one or two females. Females give birth from January to March. Between two and four cubs are born. They are weaned at around five months of age. But they usually stay with their mother for two to four years.

Polar Bear
Ursus maritimus

Length: 6½ to 9 feet
Height: to 5 feet
Weight: to 1,400 pounds
Diet: seals, seabirds, and fish; some berries or other plant material

Number of Young: 2
Home: Arctic regions
Order: carnivores
Family: bears

Arctic and Antarctic

Mammals

© TIM DAVIS / CORBIS

Endangered Animals

Most zoo visitors are familiar with the polar bear. People easily recognize its white coat and enormous size. Its natural environment is the cold Arctic region. It spends most of its time on the ice. Sometimes it must travel far to find food.

In winter, the polar bear catches seals. It uses both skill and patience to get its food. Polar bears cannot swim fast enough to catch seals underwater. But the seal is also a mammal. And it must come up through the ice for air. The bear blocks all but one of the ice holes. Then it waits quietly near the one left free. When a seal shows its head, the bear hits it very hard with its huge paw. Then it pulls the seal out of the water. Sometimes the bear goes underwater. It does so only to surprise a seal that's resting on top of the ice. The bear then emerges from the hole in the ice and chases the seal. A polar bear can run faster than 15 miles per hour. On land, the seal is too slow to escape the bear. The polar bear also captures seabirds, such as auks, and small mammals. In the summer, a polar bear eats some parts of plants, especially berries. Sometimes it also catches fish.

Several bears may gather where there is a lot of food. But they usually live alone. They meet a partner only at mating season. After mating, the female makes a large den in the snow. She keeps her young there. The polar bear has been hunted for its fat, its fur, and for "sport." Today it is protected. But it still is an endangered creature.

Bedbug
Cimex lectularius

Length: ⅛ to ¼ inch
Diet: blood
Method of Reproduction: egg layer
Home: worldwide, wherever people are found

Order: true bugs, hoppers, aphids, and relatives
Family: bed bugs

 Cities, Towns, and Farms

 Arthropods

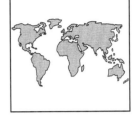

© ANTHONY BANNISTER / GALLO IMAGES / CORBIS

During the day a bedbug rests in a narrow crevice. It can be found behind a picture or light switch. Then, at night, the bedbug creeps out and crawls onto a sleeping person. It pierces his or her skin with its sharp beak, and begins to suck blood. Bedbugs eat only blood. They prefer that of humans. But if this isn't available, bedbugs will attack animals. People seldom realize that a bedbug is feeding. Symptoms—swelling and itching—appear only after the bug has returned to its hiding place. The itching is caused by the bedbug's saliva. The bedbug injects it into the skin to make it easier to suck up the blood. Bites from bedbugs may be annoying, but they are not harmful. These insects are not known to transmit any diseases.

A male bedbug can eat his own weight in blood at one meal. A female bedbug can eat almost twice her weight! She needs extra energy for laying eggs. A female bedbug lays an average of 100 to 200 eggs during her lifetime. An egg takes about a week to hatch into a tiny, partially developed nymph. The nymph passes through five stages before it becomes an adult. It molts at the end of each stage. During its lifetime a bedbug needs only six blood meals. It needs one before each molt, and one before it lays eggs. How long does it take for a bedbug to pass through these molts and become an adult? It depends on how much food is available. It may take less than two months or more than a year. The creature will not eat during this time.

Honey Bee
Apis mellifera

Length: ¾ to 1 inch (drone and queen); ½ inch (worker)
Diet: pollen and nectar
Method of Reproduction: egg layer

Home: worldwide
Order: ants, bees, wasps
Family: bumble bees, honey bees, stingless bees

 Cities, Towns, and Farms

 Arthropods

© MARTIN HARVEY / GALLO IMAGES / CORBIS

The honey bee may well be the most valuable of all insects. Each year, it produces millions of dollars' worth of honey and beeswax. Even more important is its work as a pollinator. As a honey bee settles on a flower, it collects nectar and pollen. It transfers pollen from one flower to another. This fertilizes the flowers. It also leads to the formation of fruit and seeds. What would happen if honey bees disappeared? Many kinds of plants would also disappear.

Honey bees live in highly organized colonies. The colony contains one queen bee. Her job is to lay eggs. There may be up to 60,000 sterile females in a colony. They are called worker bees. They gather food and build and guard the home. They also care for the eggs and young bees. In the summer, there may be up to 100 male bees, or drones, in the colony. Their function is to mate with the queen. Each colony lives in a hive. It contains wax combs made of six-sided cells. Some cells are used for storing pollen and honey. Other cells are used to house eggs and young bees (larvae). The queen lays as many as 2,000 eggs a day. She can live for four to five years. How many eggs do you think she can produce in that time? She can produce about 2 million eggs! When a colony becomes too big, it produces a new queen. Several larvae are fed a special food called royal jelly. One of these larvae becomes a queen. The old queen and several thousand workers then leave the hive. They establish a new colony.

Japanese Beetle
Popillia japonica

Length: ½ inch
Diet: roots (larva); leaves and fruits (adult)
Method of Reproduction: egg layer

Home: Japan, southeastern China, and eastern United States
Order: beetles
Family: scarab beetles

 Cities, Towns, and Farms

 Arthropods

© BRECK P. KENT / ANIMALS ANIMALS / EARTH SCENES

The Japanese beetle is a small, shiny green beetle. It is native to China and Japan. It is not very common in those countries because natural enemies keep its populations low. In 1916 Japanese beetles were accidentally introduced into the United States. They were found on iris roots imported from Japan. The beetles had few natural enemies in their new habitat. So they spread rapidly. They became serious pests. They damaged lawns, gardens, golf courses, and pastures. The adults feed on leaves, flowers, and fruits. The young eat the roots of grasses, vegetables, and other plants.

The life cycle of a beetle has four stages. The female Japanese beetle lays her eggs in the ground. In about a month, she lays 40 to 60 eggs. Each egg hatches into a tiny wormlike larva. This is called a grub. As they eat roots, the grubs get bigger and bigger. When autumn comes, the grubs hibernate. The following spring, they enter the pupa stage. During this time they become adults. As adults, they are ready to eat, mate, and lay eggs of their own.

Japanese beetles are kept under control by using parasites. One such parasite is the tiphiid wasp. The wasps lay their eggs on the bodies of Japanese beetle grubs. When the eggs hatch, the young wasps eat the beetle grubs.

Beluga
Delphinapterus leucas

Length: up to 18 feet
Weight: up to 3,500 pounds
Diet: fish, shrimp, lobsters, and crabs
Number of Young: 1

Home: Arctic, North Atlantic, and North Pacific Oceans
Order: dolphins, porpoises, and whales
Family: white whales

 Arctic and Antarctic

 Mammals

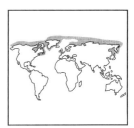

© BOB CROSLIN / CORBIS

Belugas are also known as white whales. They have adapted to life in the cold, shallow waters of the Arctic Ocean. They swim in large herds usually close to shore. The females separate from the groups to have their babies in July or August. Beluga mothers are usually six or seven years old when they are ready to mate. It takes more than a year—14 months, to be exact—for a baby beluga to develop inside its mother. When it is born, the baby is already 5 feet long! Despite its large size, a baby beluga needs its mother. It will nurse for two years. It sucks milk from nipples hidden in slits near its mother's tail. Like other mammals, belugas must breathe air to survive. Belugas can live to be 25 to 30 years old.

Belugas are hunted by humans, polar bears, and killer whales (orcas). When belugas hear orcas coming, they stop swimming and lie still in the water. The beluga's skin turns white by the time it is fully grown. This color makes it difficult for the killer whales to spot it. The beluga blends in with the color of the ice. This allows it to escape. Polar bears have developed a clever way of catching belugas. They wait at air holes that the whales have made in the Arctic ice. Belugas swimming beneath the ice must surface at these holes in order to breathe air. This makes them easy prey for polar bears, which will club the whales as they come out of the water.

Blue Bird of Paradise
Paradisaea rudolphi

Length: 2 feet
Diet: fruits, seeds, insects, and small lizards and frogs
Number of Young: 1 or 2

Home: New Guinea, Australia, and nearby islands
Order: perching birds
Family: crows, jays

 Rain Forests

 Birds

Many birds have beautiful feathers. But one family of birds has feathers so magnificent that long ago people thought they came from paradise. So they named them birds of paradise. One of the most dazzling is the blue bird of paradise.

The blue bird of paradise is related to the crow. But only its stocky body is black. It is a shiny, velvety black with some lavender, purple, maroon, and blue. Its wings and tail are the color of sparkling blue gems. Stretching outward from the bottom of its tail are delicate black feathers that are 2 feet long. At the end of each one is a jewel-like spot of color. Many of these birds were killed for their magnificent feathers. Today, the birds are protected. It is against the law to bring their feathers to the United States.

Blue birds of paradise are found in the rain forests of New Guinea. They also live on nearby islands in the southwestern Pacific Ocean. Many are found in parts of northern Australia. They eat seeds, berries, fruits, insects, and small animals. Their favorites are frogs and lizards. In this jungle habitat, the blue bird of paradise is often seen hanging straight down from a tree branch. It spreads its tail feathers into a fan-shaped rainbow of colors. One of the most important uses of the feathers is in courtship. When trying to win a female, the male will prance and dance and fluff out its feathers.

American Bison
Bison bison

Length: 10 feet
Height: 5 to 5½ feet
Weight: up to 1 ton
Diet: grasses
Number of Young: 1
Home: United States and Canada

Order: even-toed hoofed mammals
Family: antelope, bison, buffalo, cattle, goats, and sheep

 Grasslands

 Mammals

© JOE MCDONALD / CORBIS

The bison is quite an animal. It has a large body and strong front legs. It carries its large head quite low, so it appears to have a hump in its back. But a closer look shows a straight back and a neck that goes down. During the winter, the bison's coat grows long and thick. In spring, this coat becomes ragged. And the long hair disappears by summer.

Native Americans hunted bison for food and clothing. When white settlers arrived, they hunted bison, too. So there were fewer and fewer of these animals. By 1800, there were no bison east of the Mississippi River. During the mid-1800s, settlers began killing the rest of them. Many were hunted for sport. Some were killed to make way for the railroads. Others were killed in the process of clearing land for farming. Still more were killed by white settlers to starve out Native Americans. By 1889, only 541 bison were left of the original 60 million. But the animal was saved. Bison now live in large reserves in North America.

The bison eats prairie grasses. It likes dust baths. And it always takes them at the same place. Today's prairies still show where the dust baths used to be. The summer mating season begins with great fights between males looking for a mate. These fights cause injury and even death. After the mating season, the large herd splits up into smaller ones. Nine months later calves are born. The mothers nurse them for a year.

37

Red-winged Blackbird
Agelaius phoeniceus

Length: 7 to 9½ inches
Diet: insects, grain, and fruits
Number of Eggs: 3 to 5

Home: North America
Order: perching birds
Family: buntings, finches

 Freshwater

 Birds

© JOE MCDONALD / CORBIS

Fall is here, and the weather is beginning to turn cold. High in the sky, hundreds of thousands of birds—maybe a million—swarm through the air. Their bodies are black or appear to be black. But some have yellow heads; and others, purple heads. Many of them have red "shoulder patches" at the bend of their wings. These are male red-winged blackbirds. They and their relatives—yellow-headed blackbirds, Brewer's blackbirds, and others—are starting their journey south to warmer lands.

Red-winged blackbirds are one of the most common land birds in the world. They live in almost all areas of North America, especially in marshes and swamps and along the banks of streams. There the females build their nests among the reeds, cattails, and other marsh plants. Red-winged blackbirds also settle in open fields, building their nests in bushes or small trees.

Female red-winged blackbirds, which do not have the shoulder patches, lay between three and five light-blue eggs. They often have two or three broods a year and build a new nest for each one. The male does not help with the nest building or incubation, but he does help feed the chicks their daily diet of insects and grain. Blackbirds are considered pests by farmers because they eat so much grain that they can damage crops. But they also help farmers by eating harmful insects.

Eastern Bluebird
Sialia sialis

Length: 6 to 7 inches
Diet: mostly insects
Number of Eggs: 4 or 5
Home: *Summer:* eastern North America

Winter: southeastern United States and Central America
Order: perching birds
Family: Old World flycatchers

 Cities, Towns, and Farms

 Birds

© JOE MCDONALD / CORBIS

One of the best known and most loved of all birds in North America is the eastern bluebird. During the breeding season, the feathers on the male's upper parts, including his wings and tail, are bright blue. His breast and sides are reddish, and the belly is white. Females have similar, but more subdued, colors.

Eastern bluebirds have a small, slender beak. They feed mainly on beetles, grasshoppers, and other insects. Most of the insects they eat are considered pests by people, so bluebirds are very helpful to us. Bluebirds also eat other small animals and berries. People can attract eastern bluebirds to bird feeders with a mixture of peanut butter and cornmeal.

Eastern bluebirds are fine singers. Their most common call is a short *chur-lee*. The birds migrate southward in fall, then return to northern breeding grounds in early spring. For many people the return of the bluebirds means that winter is over. Bluebirds make their nests in cavities. They often use deserted woodpecker holes and hollows in decaying trees. These birds also make nests in special bluebird houses placed by people around their homes and farms. A female bluebird usually raises two groups of young each year, laying four to five pale-blue eggs each time. The young are ready to leave the nest about 19 days after they hatch.

Mountain Bluebird
Sialia currucoides

Length: 7 inches
Diet: insects and fruits
Number of Eggs: 5 or 6
Home: western North America from Alaska to central Mexico

Order: perching birds
Family: Old World flycatchers

Forests and Mountains

Birds

© GEORGE D. LEPP / CORBIS

The mountain bluebird is loved both for its beauty and its sweet song. Sadly, its low, quiet warble is growing rarer. The decline in its population can be blamed, in part, on humans. Loggers and developers have cut down many of the trees in which mountain bluebirds once nested.

To make matters worse, aggressive birds such as house sparrows and starlings compete with the bluebird for tree holes in which to build their nests. Often, mated mountain bluebirds must work together to defend their nest from sparrows, starlings, flickers, and swallows.

Fortunately, mountain bluebirds gladly adopt birdhouses erected by people. In fact, mountain bluebird chicks raised in wooden nesting boxes will look for the same type of box when they are ready to raise their own families.

Mountain bluebirds often hover over the ground as they search for ants, pill bugs, and other insects. They also dive from low branches to catch flies and mosquitoes. In winter, when insects are scarce, they eat dried berries left over from summer.

The male mountain bluebird is easy to spot in his bright blue "jacket." Although less showy, the dull brown female can be recognized by a touch of blue feathers on her rump and tail.

Bluefish
Pomatomus saltatrix

Length: 4 feet
Weight: 25 pounds
Diet: fish, notably mackerel, herring, and menhaden
Number of Eggs: unknown

Home: warm and temperate waters
Order: perch-like fishes
Family: bluefishes

 Oceans and Shores

 Fish

© JEFFREY L. ROTMAN / CORBIS

The bluefish's huge appetite has earned it a nasty reputation as a "chopping machine." Schools of bluefish attack other fish by biting and slashing at them. They can leave behind a trail of blood and injured fish miles long. Sometimes this "Cuisinart of the deep" will even attack when it's not hungry.

The bluefish fears only one predator—humans. In the United States alone, commercial fishermen catch 4 million pounds of bluefish a year. According to one count, sports fishermen catch ten times that amount! This fish is loved for its delicious taste. It also puts up an exciting fight before it is reeled in. Years ago, fishermen told tales of catching bluefish weighing 50 pounds. Today, however, the largest are about half that size.

The bluefish may actually appear silvery colored. It has a bluish or greenish back and black splotches at the base of each pectoral fin. It migrates, roaming from Florida to Maine in the warm months. It spends most of the year in tropical and subtropical waters. It was originally found only around the Americas. But in the past 50 years it has become common off the coast of France. Bluefish lay their eggs (spawn) during summer. Their eggs hatch within two days. The young grow fast. They reach about 16 inches in their first year. These young fish inherit the big appetites of their parents. They are called snappers for good reason. They feed on smaller prey near the shore.

Boa Constrictor
Boa constrictor

Length: up to 15 feet
Diet: lizards, birds, and rats
Method of Reproduction:
  live-bearer

Home: South and Central
  America
Order: scaled reptiles
Family: boas, boids

 Rain Forests

 Reptiles

© JOE MCDONALD / CORBIS

The boa constrictor is a peaceful reptile. It is not poisonous, and it doesn't attack humans. If people bother it, it just slithers away. It is also a remarkable climber.

The boa constrictor lives deep in the forests of Central and South America. It lies curled around a tree branch. It is often not noticed because its colors blend into the background. This snake is not comfortable on the ground. It moves slowly and is careful to stay away from water.

The boa stalks its prey at night. Lizards, birds, and rats are its favorite foods. Like all snakes called constrictors, it suffocates its prey. It does this while holding it by the head with its small pointed teeth. The snake's coils slowly squeeze the victim until it cannot breathe. Sometimes its heart cannot beat. Soon the prey dies. Then the snake lets go and swallows the prey whole. Its stomach juices are so strong that it can eat a porcupine and leave nothing behind but a couple of quills.

Like pythons and other boas, this constrictor has two small claws under its belly. These are the remnants of hind legs that its ancestors had. The male scratches the female with these claws before mating. The female can give birth to about 60 baby snakes at a time. They hatch as they are laid. Because of this, boa constrictors are considered live-bearers, not egg layers. The newborn snakes are 16 to 20 inches long and grow quickly.

Emerald Tree Boa
Corallus caninus

Length: 3 to 6½ feet
Diet: mainly lizards and birds
Number of Young: 10 to 18

Home: South America
Order: scaled reptiles
Family: boas, boids

 Rain Forests

Reptiles

© JOE MCDONALD / CORBIS

The emerald tree boa moves nimbly through the treetops in the Amazon rain forest. It uses its short, strong tail like a hand. The boa can thus steady its heavy body as it races along slippery branches and tree trunks. Quite suddenly it may come upon a sleeping umbrella bird. The bird awakens and tries to fly. But it has little chance of escape. The boa's mouth is like a deadly heat-sensitive missile. Temperature-sensitive pits on the boa's lips sense the warmth of the victim's body. First the boa sinks its fangs into the bird. Then it coils its body around the prey and squeezes. The bird suffocates, and the boa swallows it whole.

Feeling full and lazy, the emerald tree boa rests by looping its long, heavy body over a branch. It keeps its balance by draping several large coils of equal size on either side of the branch. Finally the boa anchors itself in place with its strong tail and relaxes. The resting boa is easy to mistake for a thick jungle vine. Many jungle birds and lizards have had the misfortune to discover this.

The boa is a vivid green on top with a yellow belly and white crossbanding. It resembles the green tree python of New Guinea and Australia. These two species live half a world apart and are only distantly related. So how did they evolve into similar forms? They live nearly identical lifestyles in almost identical environments.

Bobcat
Lynx rufus

Length: 2 to 3 feet without tail
Length of the Tail: 5 to 7 inches
Weight: 10 to 40 pounds
Diet: rodents and rabbits
Number of Young: usually 2 to 4

Home: southern Canada to central Mexico
Order: carnivores
Family: cats

 Grasslands

 Mammals

© RENEE LYNN / CORBIS

? Endangered Animals

The bobcat resembles a large house cat. It has a short tail and long legs. On its ears there are tufts of hair. Its belly is white. And its fur is brownish with black markings. Like a house cat, a contented bobcat purrs loudly. But it becomes a ferocious fighter when frightened or cornered. A bobcat screams, hisses, and spits at its enemies. And it uses its sharp teeth and claws to defend itself. With its open claws and spread-out toes, the bobcat's foot becomes very broad.

Bobcats live in many different habitats. They prefer grasslands and brushlands. But they are also found in forests, swamps, and deserts. Bobcats are active at night. Their excellent eyesight and hearing help them detect prey. They hunt for rodents, rabbits, and birds. They may even jump onto the back of a young deer and kill it. People are among a bobcat's worst enemies. They destroy its habitats and kill it for its long, soft fur.

The bobcat's home is called a lair. It can be in a hollow log, a thicket of bushes, or a rock crevice. The bobcat lines the lair with soft leaves or moss. A female bobcat gives birth to a litter of up to six kittens. The two parents care for the young together. The male bobcat often brings food for the kittens.

45